Piano • Vocal • Guitar

My Best Friend's Wedding

Interior and Back cover photos: Suzanne Tenner

ISBN 0-7935-8661-5

7777 W. Bluemound Rd. P.O. Box 13819 Milwaukee, WI 53213

Visit Hal Leonard Online at
www.halleonard.com

MY BEST FRIEND'S *Wedding*

I SAY A LITTLE PRAYER

Lyric by HAL DAVID
Music by BURT BACHARACH

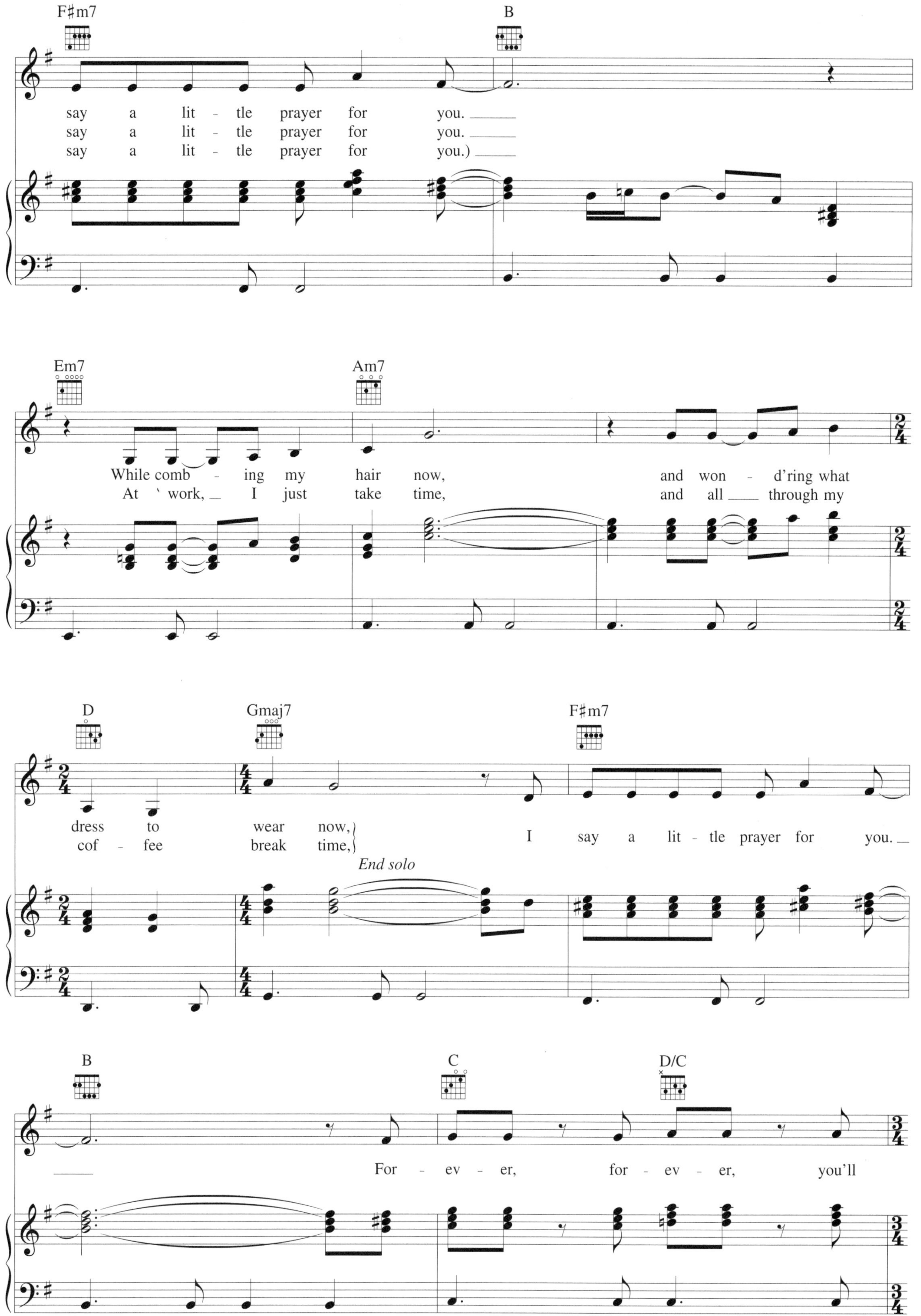
F♯m7
B
say a lit - tle prayer for you.
say a lit - tle prayer for you.
say a lit - tle prayer for you.)
Em7
Am7
While comb - ing my hair now, and won - d'ring what
At ' work, I just take time, and all through my
D
Gmaj7
F♯m7
dress to wear now,
cof - fee break time,
I say a lit - tle prayer for you.
End solo
B
C
D/C
For - ev - er, for - ev - er, you'll

Bm7
2fr
G/B
F/G
G
C
D/C
stay in my heart and I will love you. For - ev - er and ev - er, we
Bm7
G/B
F/G
G
F/G
G
C
D/C
nev - er will part. Oh, how I'll love you. To - geth - er, to - geth - er, that's
Bm7
G/B
F/G
G
C
D/C
3
how it must be. To live with - out you would on - ly mean heart - break for
B
1
2
To Coda
D.S. al Coda
me.

CODA
Em7
Am7
My dar - ling, be - lieve me,
C/D
for me there is no one but
Gmaj7
Am7/D
Gmaj7
you. Please love me, too.
Am7/D
Gmaj7
Am7/D
I'm in love with you, an - swer my

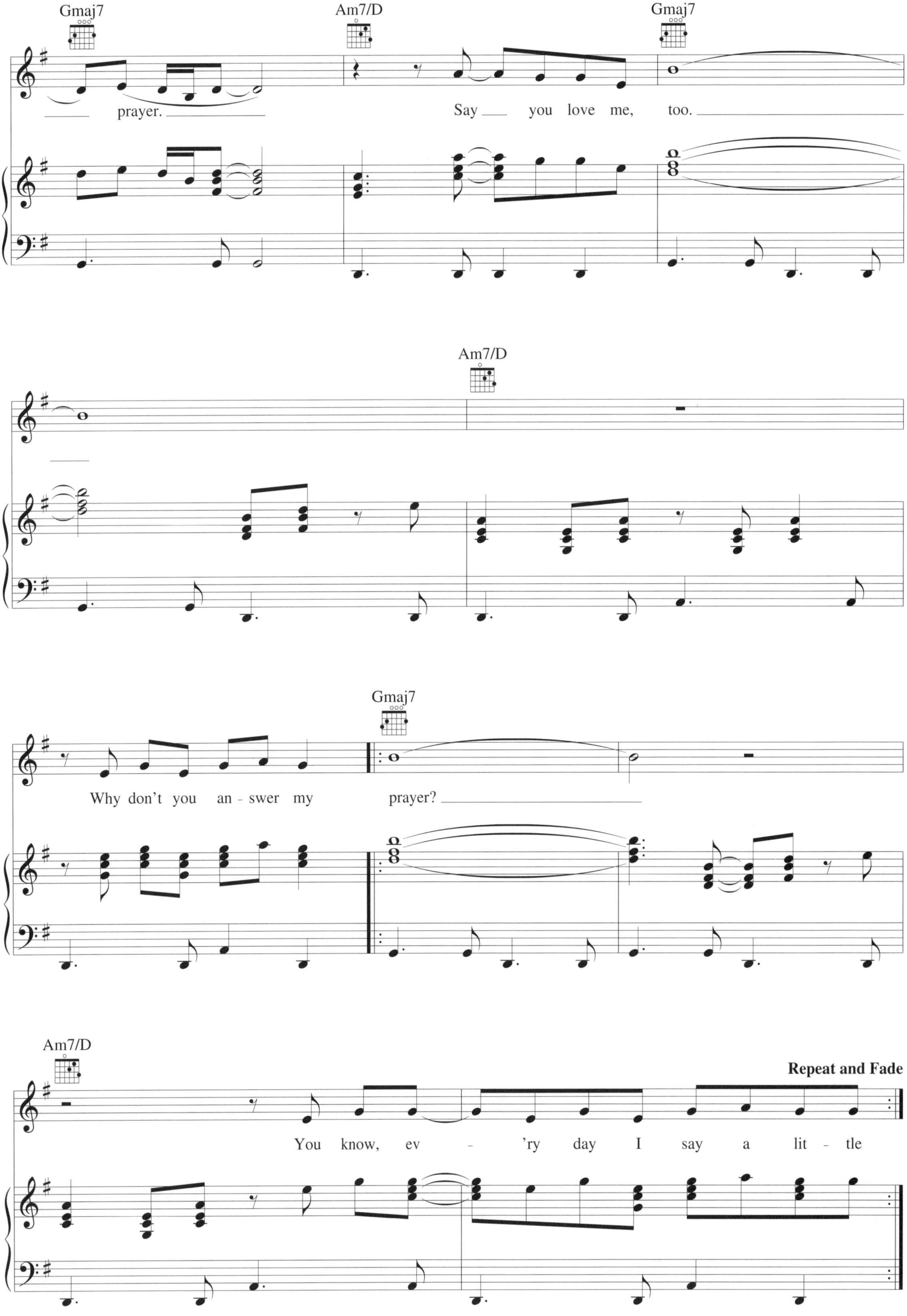

Gmaj7 Am7/D Gmaj7

prayer. Say you love me, too.

Am7/D

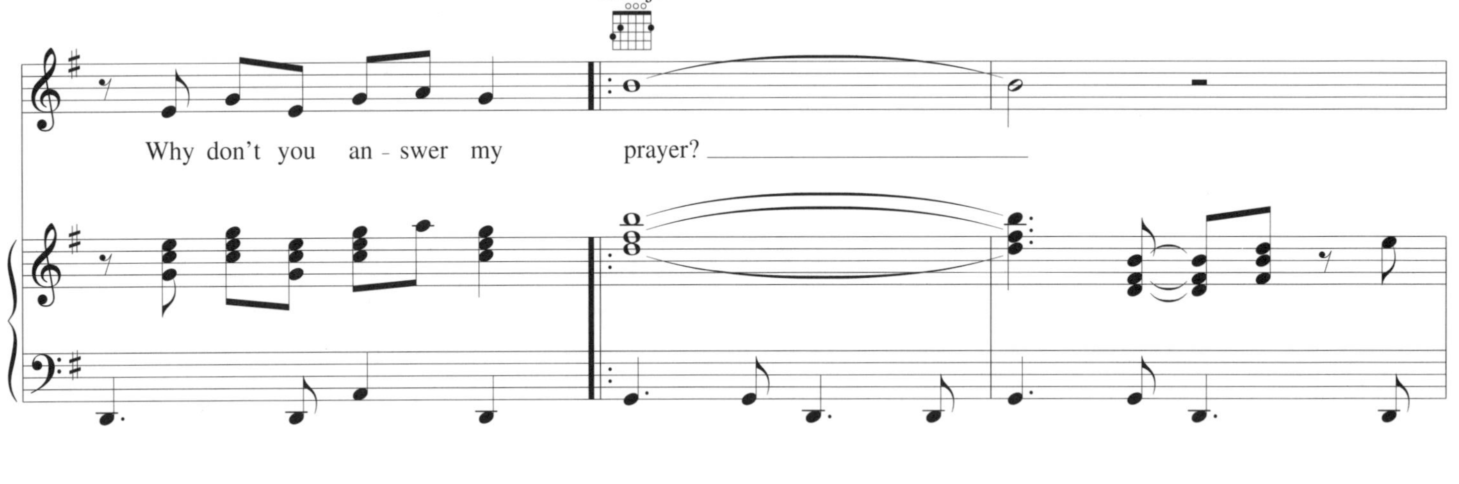

WISHIN' AND HOPIN'

Lyric by HAL DAVID
Music by BURT BACHARACH

Em
E♭
3 fr
G/D
share, all you got-ta do is hold him and kiss him and
C
D
G
C
G
N.C.
love him and show him that you care. Show him that you
D
G
care just for him, do the things that he likes to do.
D
Wear your hair just for him.

Bm
D7
'Cause you won't get him think-in' and a-pray-in', wish-in' and a-hop-in'. Just
G
G/D
C
D
wish-in' and hop-in' and think-in' and pray-in', plan-nin' and dream-in' his
kiss - es will start, that won't get you in - to his heart.
3
N.C.
B
B7
So if you're think-in' of how great true love

Em
Eb
3fr
G/D
is, all you got-ta do is hold him and kiss him and
C
D
G
D
C
C/D
Bm/D
D7
squeeze him and love him. Just do it, and af - ter you do, you will be
G
C
1
G
2
G
C
his. Show him that you You will be
G
C
G
C
G/B
Am7
G
his. You will be his.

YOU DON'T KNOW ME

Words and Music by CINDY WALKER
and EDDY ARNOLD

B♭m7
E♭7
Cm7
3 fr
F7
B♭m7
E♭7
you know me well, but you don't know me.
No, you don't
A♭
4 fr
A♭maj7
A♭7
4 fr
know the one who dreams of you at night and longs to
D♭
D♭maj7
G♭9
3 fr
kiss your lips, longs to hold you tight.
Oh, I am
A♭
4 fr
F7
B♭m7
E♭7
just a friend, that's all I've ev - er been 'cause you

A♭
G♭6
A♭
don't know me.
D♭
Ddim7
A♭/E♭
F7
(1.) I never knew the art of mak-ing love,
(D.S.) Instrumental solo
B♭m7
B♭m7/E♭
A♭
though my heart aches with love for you.
Fm
Cm7
F9
A-fraid and shy, I let my chance go by,

B♭7
E♭7
E♭7♯5
the chance that you might love me, too.
Solo ends
You give your
A♭
A♭maj7
A♭7
4 fr
hand to me, and then you say, "Good-bye." I watch you
D♭
D♭maj7
G♭9
3 fr
walk a-way be-side the luck-y guy. Oh, you will
A♭
F7
To Coda
B♭m7
E♭7
nev-er know the one who loves you so. Well, you
2

A♭
G♭6
A♭
D.S. al Coda
don't know me.
CODA
B♭m7
E♭7
N.C.
loves you so 'cause you don't know me.
A♭(add2)
G♭6
Emaj7
G♭6
Oh, no, you don't
A♭
G♭6
Emaj7
G♭
A♭
know me. Ooh, you don't know me.
molto rit.

TELL HIM

Words and Music by
BERT RUSSELL

E/B
B7
makes you want to breathe,
here's the thing to do:
if you want him to
on - ly think of you,
E
A
Tell him that you're nev - er gon - na leave him,
tell him that you're al - ways gon - na love him,
E
B7
1
E
tell him, tell him, tell him, tell him right
now.
2
E
C♯m
4 fr
now.
Ev - er since the world _ be - gan,
it's been that way for man, and

A
B7
E
wom-en were cre - at - ed to make love their des - ti - ny.
A
F#7
B7
Then why should true love be so com - pli - cat - ed? Oh yeah, uh - huh!
Em
B7
I know some - thin' a - bout love; got - ta take it
Em
B7
and show him what the world's made of, one kiss will prove it.

E
A
If you want him to be al - ways by your side,
E/B
B7
take his hand to - night, swal-low your fool - ish pride.
E
A
Tell him that you're nev - er gon - na leave him, tell him that you're al-ways gon - na love him,
E
B7
E
Repeat and Fade
tell him, tell him, tell him, tell him right now.

I JUST DON'T KNOW WHAT TO DO WITH MYSELF

Lyric by HAL DAVID
Music by BURT BACHARACH

Fm
Eb/F
Fm
Dbmaj7
Eb/Db
do - ing ev - 'ry - thing with you, plan - ning ev -
mov - ie on - ly makes me sad. Par - ties make
new love ev - er turns you down, come back; I
new love ev - er turns you down, come on back; I
Dbmaj7
Cm7
3fr
Fm
To Coda
1 Dbmaj7
- 'ry - thing for two. And now that we're through, I just don't
me feel as bad. When I'm not with you,
will be a - round, just wait - ing for you.
will be a - round, just wait - ing for you.
2,3 Dbmaj7
Abmaj7
N.C.
I just don't know what to do.
I don't know what else to do.
Like a sum - mer rose,
Eb
3fr
it needs the sun and rain.

D♭
I need your sweet
G♭
A♭
love to ease all the
E♭
1
D.S.
2
D.S. al Coda
pain.
I just don't
I don't know
CODA
D♭maj7
A♭maj7
D♭maj7

A♭maj7
D♭maj7
I'm still so cra - zy for you,
A♭maj7
D♭maj7
no, no, no, no.
I
A♭maj7
D♭maj7
don't know what else to do, I don't know what else to do, I
A♭maj7
D♭maj7
Repeat and Fade
don't know what else to do. I'm still so cra - zy for you.

I'LL BE OKAY

Words and Music by TENA CLARK
and GREG WELLS

C

no more tears to cry.
all that could have been.
you'll miss all the signs.

There's been so man-y chang-
I'll al-ways have the mem-
I've spent my life search-

Am7 C

-es. I was so con-fused.
-'ries, she'll al-ways have you.
-ing for what was al-ways there.

F G

All a-long you were the one, all the time I nev-er knew.
Fate has a way of chang-ing just what you don't want it to.
Some-times it will be too late. Some-times it won't be fair.

C 1 N.C. 2,3

I want you to be

Am7
Throw a - way the chains.
C
Am7
Let
F
C
G/B
love fly a - way.
Am7
F
C
'Til love comes a - gain,

G/B
F
Gsus
To Coda
I'll be o - kay.
C
N.C.
D.S. al Coda
Life pass - es so
CODA
F
Gsus
Am7
I won't give up, I
G/B
F
won't give in. I can't re - cre - ate what

Gsus
Am7
just might have been, but know that my heart will
G/B
Dm7
C/E
find love a - gain. Now is the time to be -
F(add9)
gin.
Am7
F
Throw a - way the chains.

C
G/B
Am7
Let
F
C
G/B
love
fly
a - way.
Am7
F
C
'Til
love
comes
a - gain,
G/B
F
Gsus
I'll
be
o - kay.

C
1
2
I
F
can't hold on for - ev - er, ba - by. Can't hold on for - ev - er, ba - by. I
C
can't hold on for - ev - er, ba - by, yeah, yeah.
F
C
I'll be o - kay.

THE WAY YOU LOOK TONIGHT

Words by DOROTHY FIELDS
Music by JEROME KERN

C13
2 fr
G♭9
3 fr
Fmaj9
Dm9
G7♭9
4 fr
you.
and the way
you look to -
Cmaj9
A7♯5(♭9)
Dm7
G6
C
Cmaj7
night.
Dm7
G7
C
Am9
Oh, but you're love - ly
Dm
G7♭9
4 fr
Gm6
3 fr
with your smile so warm
and your

Em7♭5
A7♭9
Dm7
G13
cheek so soft. There is nothing for me but
Gm7
C13
G♭9
Fmaj9
to love you, just the
Dm7
G13
C
A7♯5(♭9)
Dm7
G13
way you look to - night.
C
Am9
Fm7
Fm7/B♭
B♭9
E♭maj9
With each

Edim7
Fm7
Fm7/B♭
B♭7♭9
word your ten - der - ness grows,
E♭maj9
Cm7
3fr
Fm7
tear - ing my fear a - part.
Fm9
E9
E♭/G
3fr
Cm7♭5/G♭
And that laugh
Fm7
A♭maj7/B♭
B♭7♭5
E♭maj9
that wrin - kles your nose touch-es

Dm7
G7♭5
Cmaj9
my fool - ish heart.
Love -
Am
Dm7
Dm
G7
ly,
nev - er,
nev - er
change.
Em7♭5
A7
Dm7
Keep that
breath - less
charm.
Won't you
G13
Gm7
C13
G♭9
please
ar - range it
'cause I,
I love you

Fmaj9
Dm7
G7♭9
4 fr
Cmaj9
A7♯5(♭9)
just the way you look to - night.
Dm9
G7♭9
4 fr
Cmaj9
Dm9
G9
Mm, mm,
Dm7
G7♭9
4 fr
Just the way you look to - night.
A♭maj7
D♭maj7
Cmaj7
8va

WHAT THE WORLD NEEDS NOW IS LOVE

Lyric by HAL DAVID
Music by BURT BACHARACH

F♯m7 Bm7 G6

love, sweet love. No, not just for some,

F♯sus F♯7

but for ev - 'ry - one.

Bm7

Lord, we don't need an - oth - er moun - tain; there are
Lord, we don't need an - oth - er mead - ow; there are

Am7 D9 Gmaj7

moun - tains and hill - sides e - nough to climb.
corn - fields and wheat - fields e - nough to grow.

G6
Am7
D9
There are o - ceans and riv - ers e -
There are sun - beams and moon - beams e -
Gmaj7
Bm7
E7
nough to cross, e - nough to last 'til the end of
nough to shine. Oh, lis - ten, Lord, if you want to
A9
1 A7
Em7/A
2 A7
time. What the
know.
B♭9sus
B♭7
What the

Gm7 3fr | Cm7 3fr | Gm7 3fr | Cm7 3fr

world needs now is love, sweet love.

3

A♭6 3fr | Gm/B♭

It's the on - ly thing that there's just too

3

B♭7 | Gm7 3fr | Cm7 3fr | Gm7 3fr

lit - tle of. What the world needs now is love, sweet

Cm7 3fr | A♭6 3fr

love. No, not just for some, oh, but

Gm7
Cm7
Fm7
A♭/B♭
just for ev - 'ry, ev - 'ry, ev - 'ry -
E♭(add9)
E♭
Gm7
one.
Cm7
Gm7
Cm7
What the
Gm7
Cm7
Gm7
Cm7
Repeat and Fade
world needs now is love, sweet love. What the

I'LL NEVER FALL IN LOVE AGAIN

Lyric by HAL DAVID
Music by BURT BACHARACH

2
D/F♯
E/G♯
A
N.C.
love again.
Don't tell me what it's
E
F♯m7
E/G♯
(1.) all about 'cause I've been there and I'm
(D.S.) Instrumental solo
A
C♯m
4fr
glad I'm out,
Solo ends
out of those chains
B
To Coda
that bind you. That is why I'm

E
A
here to re - mind ___ you.
What do you get when you
F♯m7
D
fall in love? ___
You on - ly get lies,
C♯m
4fr
pain and sor - row.
So for at least ___ un -
F♯7sus
F♯7
D
E
A
D.S. al Coda
til to - mor - row,
I'll nev - er fall in ___ love.

CODA
E
A
here to re - mind you.
When you fall
F♯m7
D
in love, you on - ly get lies,
pain and sor - row.
C♯m
4 fr
So for at least un -
F♯7sus
F♯7
D
E
til to - mor - row, I'll
nev - er fall in love a - gain.

F
A
D
E
No, no, I'll nev - er fall in
D/F♯
E/G♯
A
F♯m7
love a - gain.
Oh, no.
D
Bm7
2fr
A
I'll nev - er fall in love.
(vocal 1x only)
F♯m7
D
Bm
Repeat and Fade

ALWAYS YOU

Words and Music by SOPHIE EDKVIST,
LARS HALAPI and QUINT STARKIE

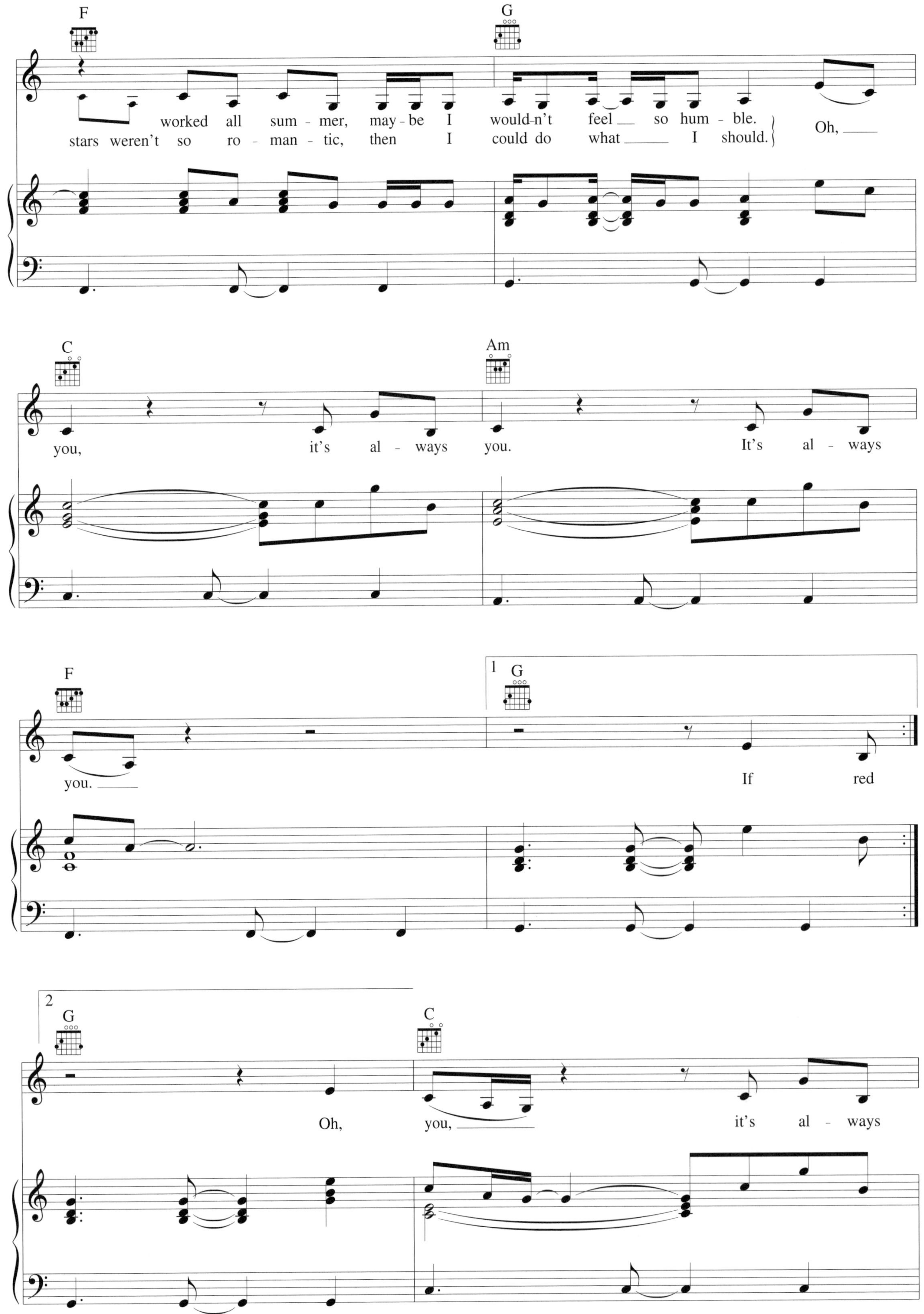
F
G
worked all sum - mer, may - be I would-n't feel so hum - ble.
stars weren't so ro - man - tic, then I could do what I should.
Oh,
C
Am
you, it's al - ways you. It's al - ways
F
1 G
you.
If red
2 G
C
Oh, you, it's al - ways

Am
F
G
you. It's al - ways you. __ If your
Am
C
love, I could com - mand __ it, get your
G
F
head to un - der - stand it, and I'd go
Am
C
twice a - round the world, __ e - ven though _

F G

I may not find it. Oh,

C Am

you, it's al - ways you. It's al - ways

F 1 G 2 G

you. Oh,

D Bm G

Instrumental solo

1
A
2
A
D
Solo ends
Oh,
you,
it's al - ways
Bm
G
1
A
you.
It's al - ways
you.
Oh,
2
A
D
Bm
G
A
D

SUITE FROM "MY BEST FRIEND'S WEDDING"

By JAMES NEWTON HOWARD

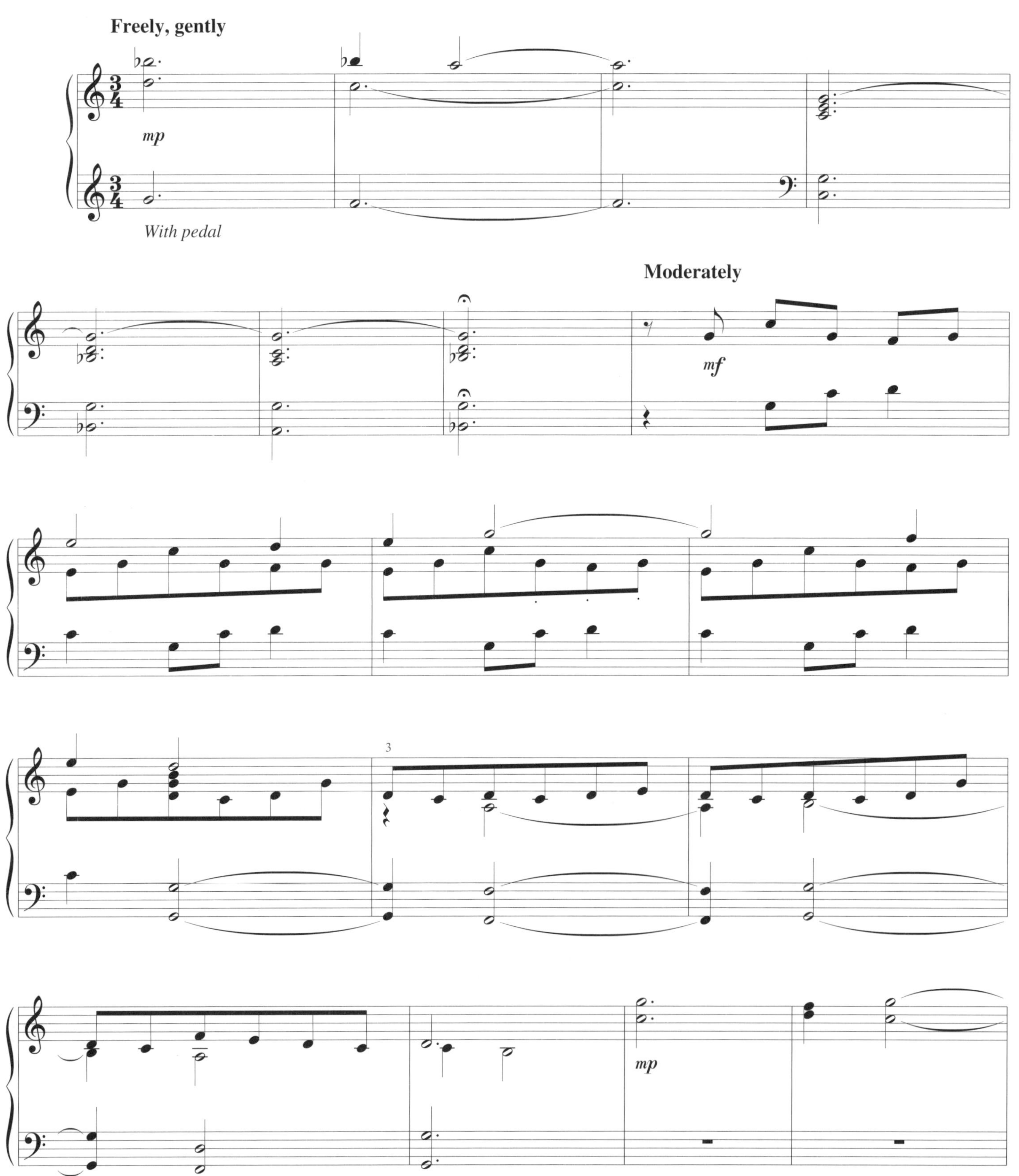

cresc.
f
2
2
2

IF YOU WANNA BE HAPPY

Words and Music by FRANK J. GUIDA,
C. GUIDA and JOSEPH ROYSTER

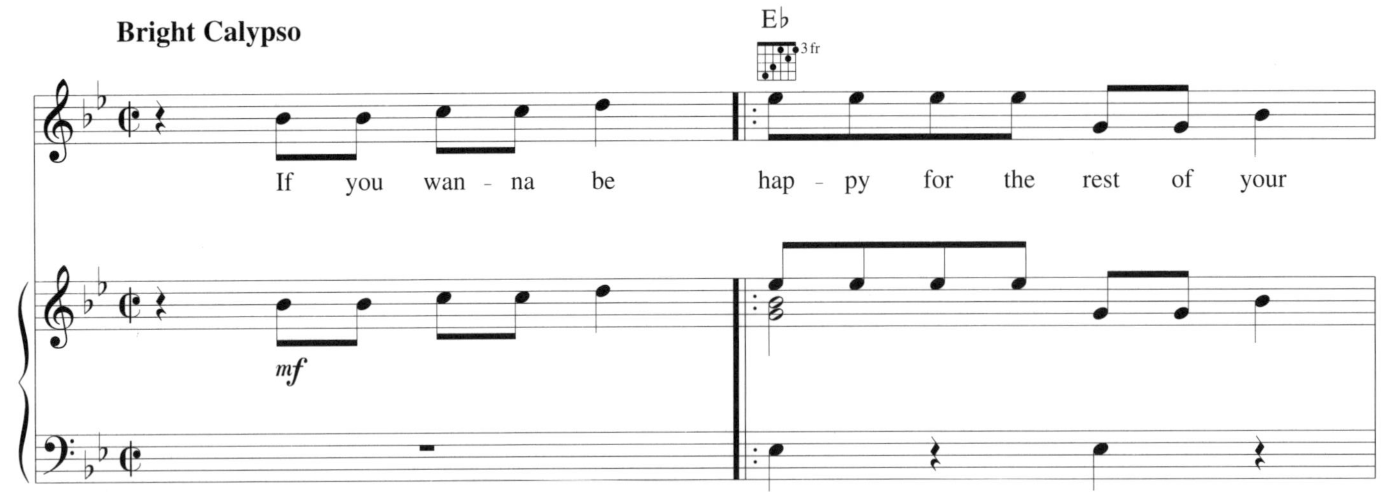

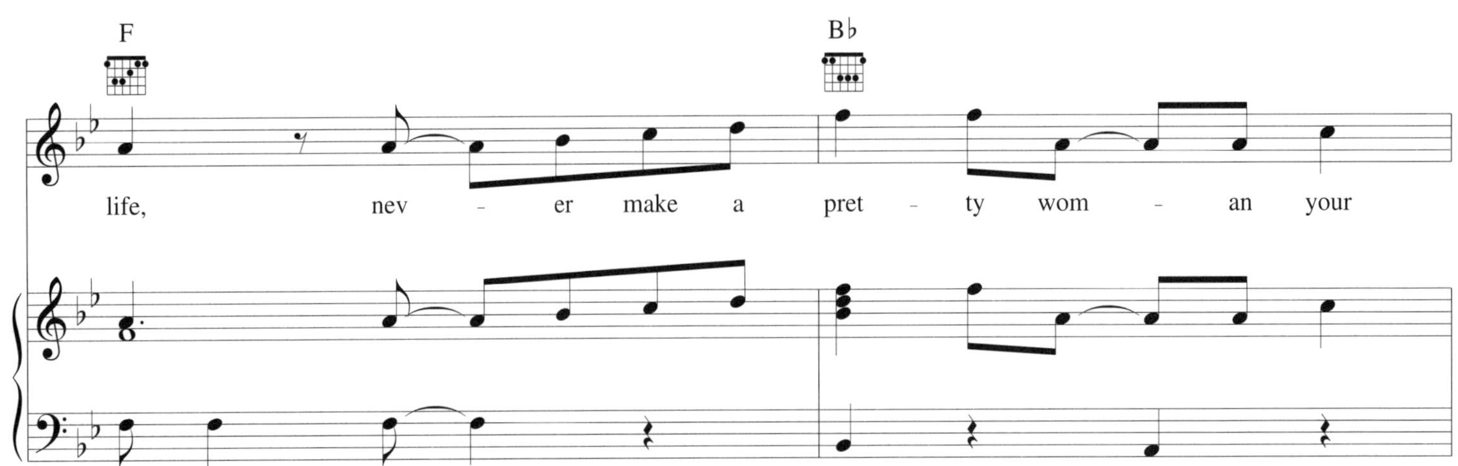

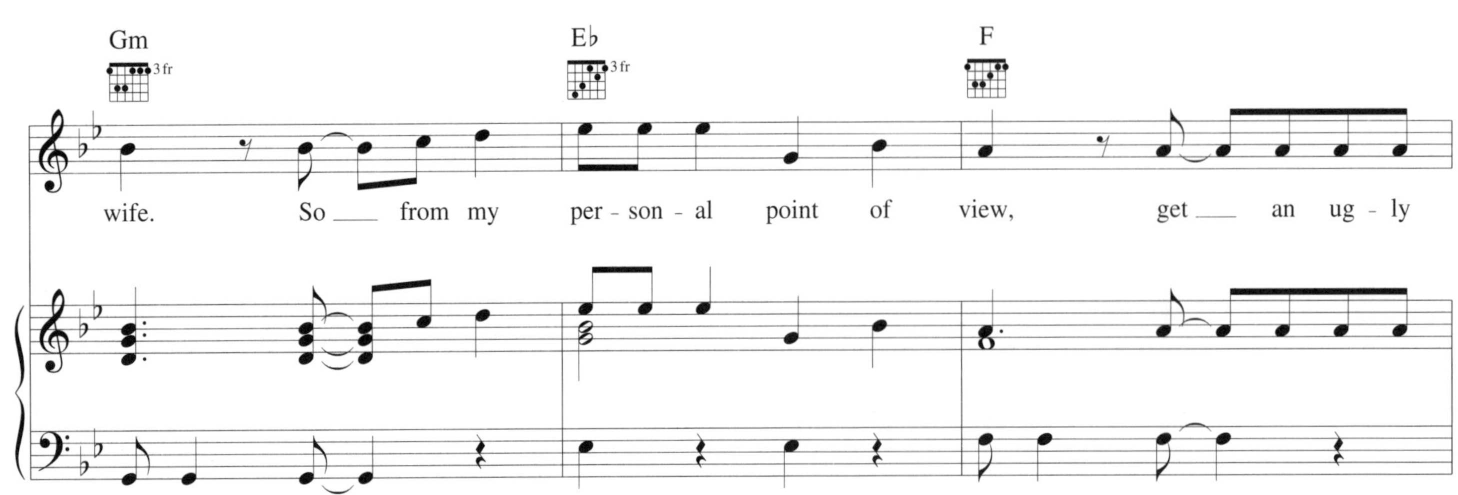

1 B♭
2 B♭
girl to mar - ry you. If you wan - na be you. A pret - ty
B♭
F7
wom - an makes her hus - band look small and ver - y of - ten caus - es his down -
make an ug - ly wom - an your wife, oh, you'll be hap - py for the rest of your
friends say you have no taste, go a - head and mar - ry an - y -
B♭
fall. As soon as he mar - ries her then she starts to do the things
life. An ug - ly wom - an cooks meals on time; she'll al - ways give
way. Though her face is ug - ly, her eyes don't match, take it from me,
F7
1 B♭
2,3 B♭
that will break his heart. But if you
you peace of mind.
she's a bet - ter catch.
If you wan - na be

E♭
3fr
F
hap - py for the rest of your life, nev - er make a
B♭
Gm
3fr
pret - ty wom - an your wife. So from my
E♭
3fr
F
To Coda
per - son - al point of view, get an ug - ly girl to mar - ry
B♭
E♭
3fr
B♭
you.
Sax solo

F7
B♭
E♭7
B♭
F7
B♭
D.S. al Coda
Solo ends
Don't let your
CODA
B♭
E♭
3fr
F
you.
Spoken: Say, man.
Yeah, baby.
B♭
Gm
3fr
E♭
3fr
I saw your wife the other day.
Yeah?
Yeah, and she's ugly.

F Bb

Yeah, she's ugly, but she sure can cook, baby! *Sung:* If you wan - na be

Eb F

hap - py for the rest of your life, nev - er make a

Bb Gm Eb

pret - ty wom - an your wife. So from my per - son - al point of

F Bb

Repeat and Fade

view, get an ug - ly girl to mar - ry you. If you wan - na be